Mark Ib[...]
Bryan S[...]

Business
START-UP 1

Workbook

CAMBRIDGE
UNIVERSITY PRESS

CAMBRIDGE UNIVERSITY PRESS
Cambridge, New York, Melbourne, Madrid, Cape Town, Singapore, São Paulo

Cambridge University Press
The Edinburgh Building, Cambridge CB2 2RU, UK

www.cambridge.org
Information on this title: www.cambridge.org/9780521672078

First published 2006
Reprinted 2006

Printed in the United Kingdom at the University Press, Cambridge

A catalogue record for this publication is available from the British Library

ISBN-13 978-0-521-53465-9 Student's Book 1
ISBN-10 0-521-53465-8 Student's Book 1

ISBN-13 978-0-521-67207-8 Workbook 1 with CD-ROM / Audio CD
ISBN-10 0-521-67207-4 Workbook 1 with CD-ROM / Audio CD

ISBN-13 978-0-521-53466-6 Teacher's Book 1
ISBN-10 0-521-53466-6 Teacher's Book 1

ISBN-13 978-0-521-53467-3 Audio Cassettes 1
ISBN-10 0-521-53467-4 Audio Cassettes 1

ISBN-13 978-0-521-53468-0 Audio CDs 1
ISBN-10 0-521-53468-2 Audio CDs 1

Contents

Introduction

Welcome to *Business Start-up* Workbook 1!

There are 12 units in the Workbook – to match the 12 units in the Student's Book.

The Workbook is designed for self-study. There is an answer key for the exercises and transcripts of the listenings at the back of the book.

Reading and writing activities

There is a wide range of activities (puzzles, wordsearches, anagrams and other exercise types) to give you new and different practice of the grammar and vocabulary in the Student's Book. You can do the activities in the Workbook after you have finished the corresponding unit in the Student's Book.

Listening activities

There is a CD of listening and speaking exercises for each unit. All these activities are 'hands free'. This means, for example, that you can listen to them in the car, or on a personal CD player, without looking at the Workbook.

Most of the speaking activities have an example to listen to first. There are pauses for you to speak, and afterwards you hear a model answer.

The CD-ROM

You can use the CD on your computer as a CD-ROM. There are extra exercises for every lesson and more chances for you to practise the language that you are learning in class.

1 **Match the pairs.**

1	Hello.	a Nice to meet you.
2	Nice to meet you.	b Yes.
3	Welcome to the company.	c Hi.
4	Are you from PKT?	d Thanks.

2 **Fill in the gaps.**

1 I'm Paul Reed and this is Julia Bell. _We're_ from CitiHomes.
2 This is David Clark. _____ from SetNet.
3 This is Alan Parker and this is Ian Dale. _____ from UN Holdings.
4 I'm George Carter. _____ from PKT.
5 This _____ Diana Edison. _____ from ST Systems.

3 **Look at the chart. Make questions and answers about the people.**

Bill	London	the UK
Anna	Hong Kong	China
Max and Anton	Berlin	Germany
Sophie	Paris	France

1 _Where's Bill from?_
  He's from London in the UK.
2 _____ ?
  _____
3 _____ ?
  _____
4 _____ ?
  _____

4 **Make four sentences. Use words from each circle.**

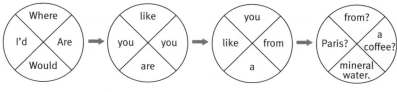

1 _Are you from Paris?_
2 _____
3 _____
4 _____

5

5 **a Look at the map. Where are the cities? Fill in the gaps.**

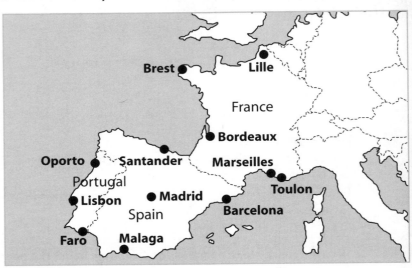

1   _Barcelona_ is in the north-east of Spain.
2   .... is in the south of Portugal.
3   .... is in the north of Spain.
4   .... is in the south of Spain.
5   .... is near Marseille.
6   .... is in the centre of Spain.

b Complete the sentences.

1 Bordeaux is _in the west of France_ .
2 Oporto is ....
3 Lille is ....
4 Brest is ....
5 Marseille is ....
6 Lisbon is ....

6 **Find the names of the drinks. Match them to the correct picture.**

| klim   fofeec   georan iceju   diec ate   pleap cijue   nelimra rewat |

1 .... _coffee_ ....   3 ....   5 ....
2 ....   4 ....   6 ....

| 1 | 2 | 3 | 4 | 5 | 6 |

7 Complete the puzzle.

Across ▶

1 Coffee with milk and
   _____?
2 Yes or _____?
3 I'd like an apple juice,
   _____ .
4 _____ is Anne Pol.
5 Germany is a _____ .
6 A coffee and a _____
   water.

Down ▼

7 _____ to ZY Holdings.
8 Could I have _____
   iced tea?
9 **A** Could I have tea, please?
   B Yes, _____ .
10 **A** An orange juice?
   B _____ , please.
11 **A** I'm from New York.
   B _____ .
12 **A** Would you like coffee?
   B No, _____ .

8 Make questions for these answers.

Ben	¹ *Where are you from?*
Sandrine	From Evry.
Ben	² _____ ?
Sandrine	It's in France, near Paris.
Ben	³ _____ ?
Sandrine	Chuck? He's from New York.
Ben	⁴ _____ ?
Sandrine	Yes, I'm from ZY Holdings in Paris.
Ben	⁵ _____ ?
Sandrine	Yes, please. Could I have a coffee?
Ben	Sure. ⁶ _____ ?
Sandrine	With milk, please. No sugar.

1 Find the words for numbers 0–10 in the puzzle. Then write the words next to the numbers.

O	N	T	F	I	V	E
T	H	H	E	E	T	O
Z	E	R	O	O	E	O
I	S	E	V	E	N	N
N	I	E	N	I	N	E
S	X	E	I	G	T	H
F	O	U	R	H	O	K
S	E	V	E	T	W	O

0 _zero_

1 _____   6 _____

2 _____   7 _____

3 _____   8 _____

4 _____   9 _____

5 _____   10 _____

2 Fill in the gaps in the quiz.

one   double   nine   seven   ten   nine   five   nine   oh

Numbers Quiz

1. The telephone number, in the UK, for fire, police and ambulance is _nine_ _____ _____ .

2. James Bond is agent _____ _____ .

3. The British Prime Minister is at _____ Downing Street, London

4. This is a Formula _____ car.

Royal Hotel ★★★★★
City Hotel ★★★
Station Hotel ★

20 roo
en Suit
Televi

5. A luxury hotel has _____ star

3 Match the pairs to make sentences.

1 What's   a time is it?
2 Is this his phone   b the next train?
3 What's your email   c this your mobile number?
4 Is   d number?
5 What   e your number?
6 When's   f address?

4 **Put the conversation in order. Write 1–6 in the boxes.**

- [ ] No, your office number.
- [1] What's your number?
- [ ] Nine eight?
- [ ] That's right.
- [ ] Oh three four seven nine eight.
- [ ] My mobile?

5 **Complete the puzzle. Write the numbers as words.**

| 80 | 16 | 7 | 11 | 17 | 20 | 19 |

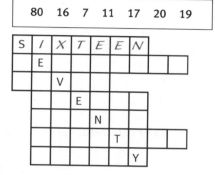

S	I	X	T	E	E	N	
	E						
		V					
			E				
				N			
					T		
					Y		

6 **Match the sentences to the pictures a–h on the menu.**

The Green Café

Sandwiches

- a £2.40
- b £2.60
- c £1.20
- d £3.80
- e £3.00
- f £2.20

Snacks

- g £2.80
- h £1.50
- i £1.00

1 A hot dog and chips, please. — *h*

2 I'd like a burger and a beef sandwich. — ___ ___

3 Would you like a chicken sandwich? — ___

4 A cheese and tomato sandwich, please. — ___

5 How much is that egg sandwich? — ___

6 Could I have one burger and two tuna sandwiches? — ___ ___

7 **Complete the word steps with the missing words.**

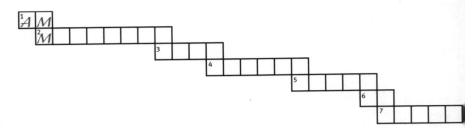

1 morning = ...
2 24.00 = ...
3 What's the ....?
4 nine, ten, ... , twelve
5 10.30 pm = ten thirty at ....
6 9.50 = ten .... nine
7 4 pm = four ....

8 **Find the mistake in each sentence. Write the correct sentences.**

1 What your telephone number?
   What's your telephone number?
2 What time it?
   ----
3 It half past ten.
   ----
4 An tuna sandwich, please.
   ----
5 Two cheese sandwich and a hot dog.
   ----
6 When the next train to London?
   ----

3 | Work

1 **Match the pairs to make jobs and workplaces. Fill in the word web with the words.**

reception-   el
account-   house
sh-   ist
technic-   op
fact-   er
engin-   ice
ware-   eer
off-   ant
manag-   ian
hot-   ory

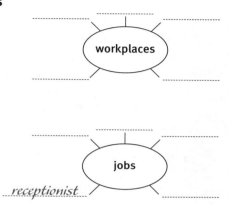

2 **Write six sentences. Choose one word from each box.**

He	We
Where	What
Do	The

do	you
live	do
company	works

has two	in
for	you
live	you

in Rome?	live?
factories.	do?
London.	HMS.

1   *He works for HMS.*
2
3
4
5
6

3 **Look at the business cards. Who are the people and what do they do?**

1 His office is in Switzerland.
  He's Bruno Evans.
  He's an engineer.

2 He works in Canada.

3 The international code for her phone number is forty-nine.

4 Her extension number is twenty-six.

Ed NELSON
Sales Manager

Montreal
+1 5144969079 (Ext 38)

Maria NOCK
Accountant
Frankfurt +49 69765743 (Ext 015)

Bruno EVANS | Engineer

Geneva +41 229448805 (Ext 204)

Anne NOTT

Technician
Singapore +65 9584322 (Ext 26)

4 **Put the conversation in order. Write 1–7 in the boxes.**

☐ I'm the manager for TopSport in Stuttgart.
☐ Nice to meet you, Simon. I'm Jan Bending.
☐ I work for SHS. I'm a sales assistant.
☐ What do you do, Jan?
☐ In their London shop?
[1] Hello. I'm Simon Fisher.
☐ Yes, and where do you work, Simon?

5 **Write the numbers on the cheques as words.**

1 *One thousand, three hundred and ninety pounds* £ 1,390

2 €48,195

3 £ 180,602

4 €1,567,000

6 **Fill in the gaps with the correct form of the verbs.**

> buy   have   own   be   work   make

1 Northgate ......*is*...... an international company.
2 Sylvia Lane .... the company.
3 We .... 75 stores in Europe.
4 120 factories all over the world .... products for Newstyle.
5 He .... for SHS.
6 They .... a lot of products from suppliers in Asia.

7 **Look at the information about Oliver and Rachel. Make six sentences about them. Use all the words in the box.**

> early   late   in the morning   at midday
> in the afternoon   in the evening

	get up	have breakfast	start work	have lunch	finish work	have dinner
Oliver	06.00	06.15	07.30	12.00	17.30	19.00
Rachel	12.30	no breakfast	21.00	14.00	06.00	20.30

Oliver
He gets up early.

Rachel

----

8 **Find the mistake in each sentence. Write the correct sentences.**

1 I gets up at six o'clock.
   I get up at six o'clock.
2 He have breakfast in a café.
   ----
3 When do you starts work?
   ----
4 Where do she have lunch?
   ----
5 What company does they work for?
   ----
6 We has dinner at eight o'clock.
   ----

4 | Information

1 **Fill in the gaps to complete the questions.**

1 _What_ does 'web' mean?

2 _____ do you spell 'Internet'?

3 _____ does 'e' stand for?

4 _____ you spell that, please?

5 _____ 'e' stand for 'electronic'?

2 **Complete the puzzle.**

1 I send and _____ ten emails a day.

2 I don't _____ this word.

3 What does this _____ ?

4 This is my _____ address.

5 _____ you speak more slowly?

6 Sorry, I don't _____ .

7 You can download this _____ .

8 I can _____ this file to a CD for you.

9 Could you say that _____ ?

10 What does 'WWW' _____ for?

11 He can read and _____ emails in English.

12 This computer downloads very _____ .

13 I'm not sure, but I _____ the letters stand for World Wide Web.

3 Make six sentences from these phrases. Use *my, your, his, her, our, their*.

company has five factories. is this
phone number?   job?   home is in Cannes.
what's   office is in Paris.   address is 4, Station Street.

1 *What's his job?* .... He's an engineer.
2 She works in France. ....
3 I live in the town centre. ....
4 They live in France on the coast. ....
5 .... No, it's Jack's.
6 .... We make products for the home.

4 Fill in the gaps in the email.

Email   Extension   From   Subject   Thank   Best   Tel.   To   Dear

1 *To* : **Jacky Fogden**
2 .... : **Klaus Ziegert**
3 .... : **IT Training course**

4 .... Jacky,

5 .... you for your message. You are very welcome on the IT Training Course. Could you send me your office number and the number of your extension, please?

6 .... regards,

PS. Could you also send me a copy of your CV?

Klaus Ziegert

Training Manager-KP Systems
7 .... : **k.ziegert@kpsystems.de**
8 .... : **+49 8561 8244**   9 .... : **226**

5 **Fill in the gaps.**

> hard drive   download   software   website   book
> credit card   send   copy   print   mail

1 You can read e-books with this _software_ .
2 Can you buy plane tickets from this _____?
3 You receive the tickets by _____ .
4 I _____ about 30 emails a day.
5 You can _____ a hotel by phone or online.
6 I can't _____ this file from their website.
7 Can I pay by _____ _____ ?
8 I can _____ this document onto a disk for you.
9 That file is on the computer's _____ _____ .
10 Can you _____ a copy of the report for me?

6 **Find the mistake in each sentence. Write the correct sentences.**

1 What do you spell that?
   How do you spell that?
2 You could speak slowly, please?
   ----
3 What's Jan number?
   ----
4 What's the number to the Paris office?
   ----
5 I no open the file.
   ----
6 You can to download music from the Internet.
   ----

5 | Places

1 Find the names of the office equipment and furniture. Match them to the pictures.

hoitoprepco	rentpri	pilf tharc	bleta	crihas	axf hemanci

1 _____table_____   3 _____   5 _____

2 _____   4 _____   6 _____

1   2   3   4   5   6

2 Look at the meeting room. Fill in the gaps with *there is/are* or *there isn't/aren't* to make true sentences.

1 _____There are_____ four power sockets and a printer.

2 _____ a flip chart.

3 _____ five chairs.

4 _____ six chairs.

5 _____ a laptop.

6 _____ two computers and a laptop.

7 _____ a photocopier.

8 _____ three power sockets.

17

3 **What am I?**

My first letter is in 'file', but not in 'first'.
My second letter is in 'fax', but not in 'five'.
My third letter is in 'copy', but not in 'slowly'.
My fourth letter is in 'can't', but not in 'can'.
My fifth letter is in 'room', but not in 'meeting'.
My sixth letter is in 'pay', but not in 'buy'.
I'm a _f_ _ _ _ _ _ .

4 **Complete the puzzle with words about property.**

						1 D	O	O	R			
2						O						
	3					W						
4						N		■				
						5 S						
		6				T						
	7					A						
			8			I						
			9			R						
		10				S						

1 You go into a room through this.
2 You have a bath here.
3 You look through this.
4 You swim in it.
5 This flat has only one room.
6 You go out of a building through this.
7 You go into a building through this.
8 You see this when you look out of a window.
9 This word means 'houses' and 'flats'.
10 You go downstairs from the ground floor into this.

5 **Write the opposites.**

1 modern   _old_
2 high   ....
3 small   ....
4 horrible   ....
5 cold   ....
6 expensive   ....

6 **Find the mistake in each sentence. Write the correct sentences.**

1 Are there a photocopier?
   Is there a photocopier?

2 There isn't phone sockets in the room.

3 I need to phone to my office.

4 The toilets are over there in the right.

5 The rooms are very bigs.

6 My office is on the six floor.

7 **Start from the entrance. Follow the directions. Where are you?**

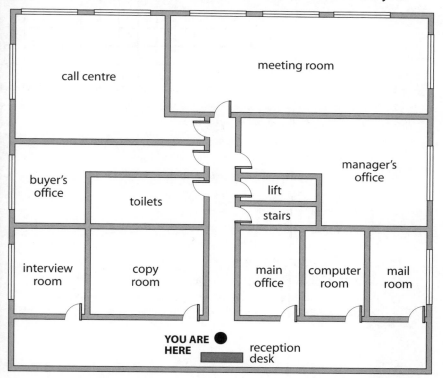

1 Go to the end of the corridor.   *the meeting room*
2 They're on the left after the copy room.
3 Turn left. It's the second room on the right.
4 It's just past the stairs.
5 Turn right. It's the third room on the left.

6 | Action

1 Complete the puzzle.

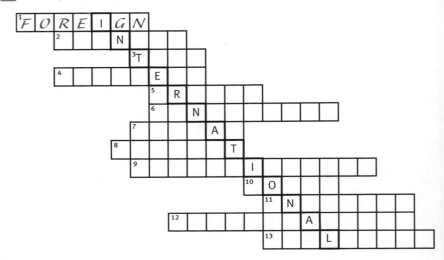

1 I often phone _____ customers, but they can usually speak English

2 Poland is a _____ in Eastern Europe.

3 I like working with other people, in a _____ .

4 I often go on _____ trips.

5 I sometimes _____ to Europe for my job.

6 I go to the sales _____ every year.

7 I don't often go _____ on business.

8 We are working on a new _____ .

9 Emails and cheap phone calls make _____ very easy.

10 Modern telecommunications make the _____ a small place.

11 I always buy tickets on the _____ .

12 I don't often give _____ to large groups.

13 I'm working with a _____ on this project. She works in my department.

2 **Add the adverbs to the sentences.**

1 He goes on business trips. *(never)*
   He never goes on business trips.

2 We go to conferences. *(often)*
   _____

3 I am in the office in the afternoon. *(always)*
   _____

4 She doesn't give presentations in English. *(usually)*
   _____

5 They have meetings in my office. *(sometimes)*
   _____

3 **Complete the sentences about the picture. Use the present continuous of the verbs in the box.**

| write   eat   drink   speak   make   work   send   read |

1 Two men *are speaking* on the phone at the moment.
2 One man _____ a sandwich.
3 One man _____ at a computer.
4 One woman _____ a report.
5 One man _____ a newspaper.
6 One woman _____ a photocopy.
7 Two people _____ coffee.
8 One woman _____ a fax.

4 Write the names of the activities under the pictures.

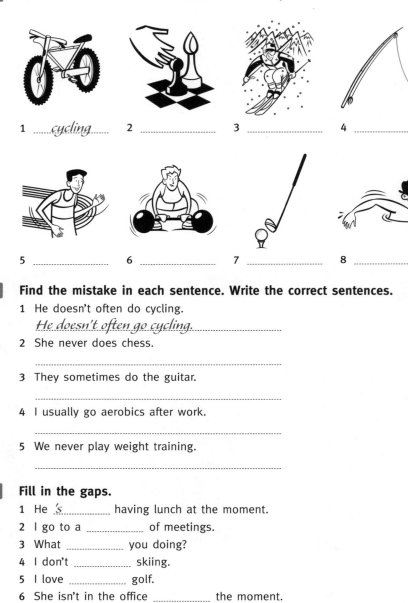

1 _cycling_ 2 _____ 3 _____ 4 _____

5 _____ 6 _____ 7 _____ 8 _____

5 Find the mistake in each sentence. Write the correct sentences.

1 He doesn't often do cycling.
   He doesn't often go cycling.

2 She never does chess.
   _____

3 They sometimes do the guitar.
   _____

4 I usually go aerobics after work.
   _____

5 We never play weight training.
   _____

6 Fill in the gaps.

1 He _'s_ having lunch at the moment.
2 I go to a _____ of meetings.
3 What _____ you doing?
4 I don't _____ skiing.
5 I love _____ golf.
6 She isn't in the office _____ the moment.
7 I'm not very good _____ cooking.
8 He's not here. He's working in the Milan office _____ week.

7 | Meeting

1 Complete the puzzle with the months of the year.

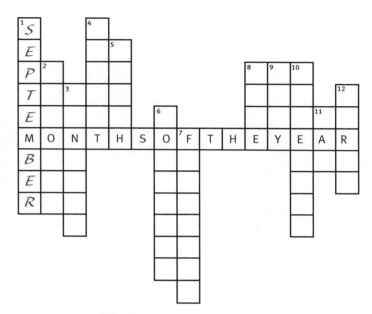

2 Find the days of the week.

1 dafiry   _Friday_
2 yodman   ....
3 nudysa   ....
4 sudeaty   ....
5 thudrays   ....
6 rastuday   ....
7 dewdanesy ....

3 **Fill in the table with the time expressions.**

the afternoon   the 10th
the end of January   Monday
the 6th   the end of the month
the beginning of the week   the 21st August
April   July
night   the middle of the month

at	on	in
		the afternoon

4 **Match the pairs.**

1 When can we meet?
2 Are you free at the end of August?
3 When are you free?
4 What about Friday the 10th?
5 I can make it on the 15th June. Is that OK?

a Friday? Yes, that's fine.
b No, I'm busy in the middle of the month.
c No, I'm very busy then.
d What about the 26th April?
e I'm free in the first week of July.

5 **Put the words in order. Then match the questions to the answers.**

1 leaving / he / when's ?
   When's he leaving?
2 she / how's / travelling ?
   ----
3 she / is / direct / flying ?
   ----
4 are / when / you / back / coming ?
   ----
5 taking / the / are / train / you ?
   ----
6 staying / are / where / they ?
   ----
7 they / are / who / meeting ?
   ----
8 train / is / why / going / she / by ?
   ----

a I'm returning on Friday.

b No, she's changing in London.

c The manager.

d Next week.

e By plane.

f No, I'm flying.

g She doesn't like flying.

h In New York.

6 **Fill in the gaps.**

1 **A** When does the next train leave?

   B Sorry, I don't have a t*imetable* .

2 I'd like to cancel my r_____ for the 9.30 train to London.

3 How much is the standard f_____ to London?

4 I want to reserve a s_____ on the 8.15 train to Liverpool.

5 Would you like a single or a r_____ ticket?

6 Do you want to travel f_____ class or standard class?

7 Do you want to b_____ the return trip now?

8 Just a s_____ ticket, please.

7 **Find the mistake in each sentence. Write the correct sentences.**

1 I'm free in the beginning of the month.

   I'm free at the beginning of the month.

2 Are you busy at Monday?

   _____

3 What are you do next week?

   _____

4 I'm take the train to Paris next Monday.

   _____

5 I want travel first class.

   _____

6 I like to book a seat.

   _____

8 | Reporting

1 Put the words in order from the past to the future.
Number the boxes 1–11.

☐	this afternoon	☐	last year
☐	this morning	☐	three days ago
☐	yesterday	☐	a week ago
☐	ten years ago	1	a hundred years ago
☐	tomorrow	☐	this evening
☐	last month		

2 Find the mistake in each sentence. Write the correct sentences.

1 He weren't at the meeting.
He wasn't at the meeting.

2 They was in India.

3 She were at the trade fair.

4 Was you at the training course?

5 They wasn't in the office last week.

6 We was late this morning.

7 Were the meeting very big?

3 Put the words in order. Then match the questions to the answers.

1 the / was / meeting / how ?
How was the meeting?

a Last week.

2 how / were / fair / at / many / the / companies / trade ?

b No, it was small.

3 was / the / conference / when ?

c The sales team.

4 was / the / training / at / who / course ?

d About five hundred

5 the / was / where / conference ?

e It was in Boston.

6 conference / the / was / big / very ?

f It was good.

4 **Complete the email with these phrases.**

a really big conference with over 3,000 visitors.   was fantastic.

a copy of my report for your information.

also a very good exhibition with lots of new books and new technology.

my trip to Milan.   lots of very good talks and presentations.

Hi Josh,

I'm back in the office again after *my trip to Milan.*

The conference _____

There were _____

There was _____

It was _____

Here is _____

Regards,

Tony

---

5 **Make five sentences. Use words from each circle.**

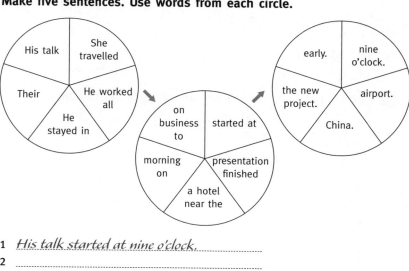

1 *His talk started at nine o'clock.*

2 _____

3 _____

4 _____

5 _____

27

6 **Find past tenses in the puzzle and fill in the chart.**

```
D R O V E M A
S C U P S A W
B O U G H T C
W S H H A D A
E T O O K E M
N F L E W T E
T E (L E F T) L
```

	infinitive	past tense
1	to leave	*left*
2	to fly	
3	to buy	
4	to come	
5	to have	
6	to take	
7	to cost	
8	to drive	
9	to go	
10	to see	

7 **Fill in the gaps.**

> beach   nightlife   sightseeing   hotel
> apartment   coach   holiday   ferry

1 Did you have a good *holiday* ?
2 I rented an _____ .
3 He relaxed on the _____ .
4 The _____ was great – lots of discos and restaurants.
5 They went on a tour of the island by _____ .
6 We took a _____ to the next island.
7 Did you go _____?
8 The receptionist at our _____ was very friendly.

8 **Make questions for the <u>underlined</u> words in the answers.**

1 *Did you rent a car* _____?
  <u>Yes</u>, we rented a car.
2 _____?
  We flew to Goa <u>on Monday</u>.
3 _____?
  We travelled <u>by car</u>.
4 _____?
  We stayed in Paris <u>for two days</u>.
5 _____?
  <u>Yes</u>, he went to China last month.
6 _____?
  <u>Yes</u>, they had a really good holiday.

1 **Fill in the diagram with the names of documents.**

> graph   agenda   bar chart   table   minutes   schedule   pie chart

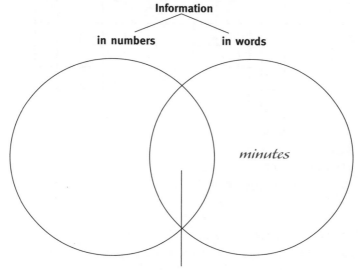

Information

in numbers   in words

minutes

in numbers or words

2 **Find the mistake in each sentence. Write the correct sentences.**

1 Could you send I an email?

   Could you send me an email?

2 What time can I phone they?

   ----

3 I emailed Tom and sent he a copy of the report.

   ----

4 I called she at the office.

   ----

5 I need a copy of the minutes. Could you send one to I?

   ----

6 We need to discuss this with you. Could you call we?

   ----

7 Where are Sam and Tony? I need to speak to they.

   ----

3 **Complete the telephone puzzle.**

¹H	O	¹⁰L	D

Across ▶
1 Would you like to .... ?
2 Sorry, could you say that .... ?
3 Could you take a .... ?
4 Sorry, I'm .... he's out.
5 Could you ask him to call me .... ?
6 Could you .... her a message, please?

Down ▼
5 His line's .... at the moment.
7 Could I .... to Max, please?
8 Who's .... , please?
9 Could I .... your name again?
10 Her .... 's busy.

4 **Make four sentences. Use words from each box.**

I think	Taking a person's		taking a person's	back is		name is quite easy.	a colleagu is very difficult.
I think taking	Asking a person to call		phone number	a message for		very easy.	is quite difficult.

1 *I think taking a person's name is quite easy.*
2 ....
3 ....
4 ....

5 Look at the weather map of the UK. What's the weather like? Fill in the gaps.

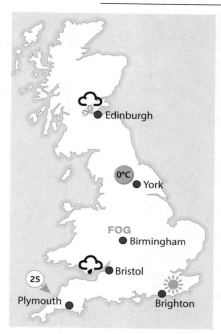

| foggy | freezing | sunny |
| snowing | windy | raining |

1 It's _freezing_ in York.
2 It's _____ in Bristol.
3 It's _____ in Birmingham.
4 It's _____ in Brighton.
5 It's _____ in Edinburgh.
6 It's _____ in Plymouth.

6 Find the mistake in each sentence. Write the correct sentences.

1 The weather is horrible last night.
   The weather was horrible last night.
2 It rains all day yesterday.
   ----
3 It snows at the moment.
   ----
4 What does the weather like?
   ----
5 In April we often are getting a lot of rain.
   ----
6 Last week it were windy and cold.
   ----
7 In Moscow it freezing today.
   ----
8 It was a thunderstorm in Orlando last week.
   ----

1 **Find nine adjectives in the puzzle.**
Write them next to their opposites.

1 old   _modern_
2 difficult   ....
3 cheap   ....
4 long   ....
5 bad   ....
6 slow   ....
7 high   ....
8 dangerous   ....
9 small   ....

M	S	H	O	R	T	V	E	M
A	D	D	O	O	F	I	L	O
N	E	E	S	E	A	S	Y	D
E	X	P	E	N	S	I	V	E
L	L	O	W	E	T	S	O	R
G	O	O	D	E	R	A	K	N
O	N	E	E	L	A	F	I	N
M	P	L	A	R	G	E	S	G

2 **Find the mistake in each sentence. Write the correct sentences.**

1 A train is more long than a bus.
   A train is longer than a bus.

2 A Ford is cheapest than a Rolls Royce.
   ....

3 This old fax machine is worser than that new one.
   ....

4 Economy class is less expensiver than business class.
   ....

5 A sports car can go more fast than a bus.
   ....

6 This modern laptop is more small than that computer.
   ....

7 This is the more difficult question in the book!
   ....

8 You always have the better ideas.
   ....

3 **Read the discussion in a meeting and fill in the gaps.**

agree   right   true   sure   think

Mary OK. The first thing on the agenda is the conference. The second is the new project and item three is the sales figures, if we have time.

Tom I ¹ _agree_ that the conference is important, but I ² _____ we need to talk about the sales figures first.

Mary Hmm. I'm not so ³ _____ . You're ⁴ _____ that the sales figures are important, but we must have a plan for the project before we go to the conference.

Tom Yes, that's ⁵ _____ . OK. Let's do that, then.

4 **Make five sentences. Use phrases from each box.**

Twenty years ago planes	way to	travel from London to Paris is by train.
Today the fastest	to travel for long distances is	is by car.
The TGV is the	were the most	by bus.
The most	convenient way to travel	cities in France.
The least comfortable way	quickest way to travel between	expensive way to travel.

1 _Twenty years ago planes were the most expensive way to travel._
2 _____
3 _____
4 _____
5 _____

5 Sense or nonsense? Change the nonsense sentences so that they make sense. (Sometimes there is more than one way to do this.)

		S	N
1	The flight to Berlin is now boarding. The flight is delayed.	☐	✓
2	The flight to London is cancelled. The check-in is now open.	☐	☐
3	The Paris flight is on time. It's thirty minutes late.	☐	☐
4	The flight to Singapore is boarding. The check-in is now closed.	☐	☐
5	There's no flight to Bangkok. Passengers are getting onto the plane.	☐	☐
6	The flight to New York is delayed. The expected departure is now 14.00.	☐	☐

1 The flight to Berlin is now boarding. The flight is on time.

----

6 Fill in the gaps with *some*, *any* or *no*.

1 **A** Do you have __*any*__ luggage?
  B No, just this briefcase.
2 **A** Are there _____ window seats left?
  B Yes, there are _____ at the back of the plane.
3 **A** Do you have _____ other bags?
  B No, I have _____ other bags.
4 **A** Are there _____ shops after the security check?
  B Yes, there are _____ shops near the restaurant.
5 **A** Are there _____ cafés over there?
  B No, there are _____ cafés at the gate.

7 Fill in the gaps.

1 I prefer __*to*__ fly.
2 Small, new cars are _____ economical than big, old ones.
3 _____ cheapest way to travel is by bicycle.
4 The flight is _____ time.
5 Modern trains are faster _____ old ones.
6 I'm _____ so sure about that.

11 | Plans

1 Find the sequencing words. Then fill in gaps in the plans.

hetn   faert   nlfiayl   tnxe   srtif

1 _First_ we're going to plan the report.
2 _____ coffee we're going to write the report.
3 _____ we're going to email the report to everyone in the team.
4 _____ we're going to discuss the report at our 5_____ team meeting.

2 Make five sentences. Use words from each circle.

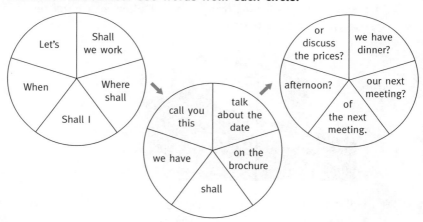

1 _Let's talk about the date of the next meeting._
2 _____
3 _____
4 _____
5 _____

3 Find words with the letter *T*. Fill in the gaps.
1 Let's look at the _p h o t o s_ for the new brochure.
2 There's lots of useful information on this _ _ _ _ _ t _.
3 What's the name of their new _ _ _ _ _ _ t?
4 What shall we discuss _ _ _ t?
5 What's the _ _ t _ of the next team meeting?
6 We must do this first. It's very _ _ _ _ _ t.
7 I think it's _ _ _ _ _ t _ _ t to do this first.
8 Let's discuss the report _ _ t _ _ lunch.

4 **Find two mistakes in each sentence. Write the correct sentences.**

1 They're going look at the brochure week.

   They're going to look at the brochure next week.

2 Are you go to make changes at the website?

----

3 He goes to discuss the new project this tomorrow.

----

4 They going call the office later.

----

5 We're going not to have design ready for the meeting.

----

5 **Make seven sentences from a conversation at a hotel reception. Use words from each column.**

1 I've got a	paying the	out, please?
2 Could you	I check	form, please?
3 Can you put	a wake-up	here, please?
4 This card	is the key for	call?
5 Would you like	reservation for	your room.
6 Could	your signature	bill.
7 My company's	fill in this	a double room

1 *I've got a reservation for a double room.*

2 --

3 --

4 --

5 --

6 --

7 --

6 **Put the conversation in the correct order. Number the boxes 1–9.**

- [ ] Thanks.
- [ ] Could you tell me your names, please?
- [ ] For two nights?
- [ ] Yes, that's right.
- [ ] Sure. Briggs and Wood.
- [ ] OK. Rooms 203 and 204 on the second floor. Here are your keys.
- [ ] Could you fill in this form, please?
- [ ] Of course.
- [1] Hello. We've got a reservation for two single rooms.

7 **Fill in the gaps with the correct form of *have got*.**

1 I *'ve* got a reservation.
2 _____ you got a key?
3 No, I _____ got a pen.
4 The hotel _____ got a restaurant.
5 You _____ got a message from your office.

8 **Find the hotel words. Then match them to the definitions a–g.**

1 kecch uto   *check out*
2 libl   _____
3 inbiram   _____
4 tredic drac   _____
5 texsar   _____
6 moro viserec   _____
7 pionerecsitt   _____

a You can find this in your hotel room.
b This person works in the hotel.
c These are phone calls, drinks and snacks, for example.
d You do this when you leave a hotel.
e You use this to pay.
f You pay this when you leave.
g When the hotel delivers food or drink to your room.

1 **Fill in the gaps.**

> increased   costs   loss   sales   profit margin
> decreased   improve   quarter

Sally O'Sullivan
managing director of a car hire company.

> Our business is doing really well. The company's sales
> ¹ *increased* by 20% last ² _____ .

Karl Becker
manager of a furniture factory in Dortmund, Germany.

> Our ³ _____ _____ is very low at the
> moment. The main problem is that the euro is high.
> That makes our products more expensive for people
> from the US, Japan and Eastern Europe. Our sales
> ⁴ _____ by 15% last quarter.

Serge Debré
estate agent in Dieppe, France.

> Last year was a very difficult year for us. Our
> ⁵ _____ of holiday homes to English buyers were
> very low. We made a big ⁶ _____ . We must cut
> our ⁷ _____ to ⁸ _____ our business!

2 **Fill in the gaps with *much* or *many*.**

1 Did the new customer order _____*many*_____ laptops?
2 How _____ stores are selling this product?
3 Did you make _____ profit last month?
4 How _____ discount are they giving?
5 Is there _____ demand for this photocopier?
6 Do _____ people work in the warehouse?

3 **Find two mistakes in each sentence. Write the correct sentences.**

1 At the moment our company does quite bad.
   At the moment our company is doing quite badly.

2 My colleagues works very hardly.

   ....

3 Business improve quick last year.

   ....

4 It's not good for businesses grow fastly.

   ....

5 Our sales is increasing slow.

   ....

4 **Complete the puzzle.**

1 We .... with two other companies.
2 There's a big .... for this product.
3 We have three big .... in this market.
4 My local .... sells over a thousand different products.
5 There's a lot of .... in this market.
6 Our product is good quality and not expensive. It's very .... !
7 We made 20% .... last year.
8 Everything was 50% .... in the sale.
9 They have good jobs. They .... £100,000 a year.
10 Our supplier gives us a 10% .... on all orders.
11 Can I .... by phone?
12 We have lots of .... in the warehouse at the moment.

5 Fill in the gaps with *this*, *that*, *these* or *those*.

1

Can I try on _those_ jeans, please?

2

How much is _____ watch?

3

I like _____ shoes.

4

Is _____ T-shirt in the sale?

6 Fill in the gaps.

size	receipt	off	changing	pin number	sale	cash	medium	try

1 This store has a winter and a summer ____ *sale* ____ .
2 There's twenty percent _____ all prices.
3 **A** Can I _____ this on?
  B Yes, the _____ room is over there.
4 **A** What's your _____ ?
  B Ten, I think.
5 I don't have any _____ . Can I pay by credit card?
6 Could I have a _____ , please?
7 Do you know the _____ for your credit card?
8 What's your size? _____ or large?

7 Put the conversation in a shop in order. Number the boxes 1–9.

☐ Yes, of course. What's your size?

☐ Yes, fine. I'll take them. Can I pay by credit card?

☐ Yes, please. How much do these shoes cost? I can't find the price.

☐ Can I try them on?

1 Do you need any help?

☐ I'm a size 43. That's size 10 in the UK, I think.

☐ They're £50 now. They were £90.

☐ Yes, no problem.

☐ Yes. That's right. Here you are. ... Are they OK?

Transcripts

Unit 1

▶▶ **1** **Listen to the conversation.**

A Hi, I'm Isabelle.
B *Hello, I'm Tom. Nice to meet you.*
A Nice to meet you. Welcome to Paris.
B *Thanks.*

Listen again and reply for you.

▶▶ **2** **Make sentences. Listen to the example.**

from London

I   *I'm from London.*
he   *He's from London.*
she   *She's from London.*
you   *You're from London.*
we   *We're from London.*
they   *They're from London.*

▶▶ **3** **Listen to the conversation.**

A Where are you from?
B *I'm from Saltdean.*
A Where's that?
B *It's in the south of England, near Brighton.*
A Right.

Listen again and reply for you.

▶▶ **4** **Listen to the conversation.**

A Would you like a drink?
B *Yes, please. Could I have a coffee?*
A OK. Milk? Sugar?
B *Sugar, please. No milk, thanks.*

Listen again and reply. Ask for a coffee.

Unit 2

▶▶| **5** **Ask questions. Listen to the example.**

what's your / number
What's your number?

phone number
What's your phone number?

address
What's your address?

mobile number
What's your mobile number?

fax number
What's your fax number?

email address
What's your email address?

▶▶| **6** **Say the times. Listen to the example.**

two	*It's two o'clock.*
three	*It's three o'clock.*
five	*It's five o'clock.*
ten	*It's ten o'clock.*
five past eight	*It's five past eight.*
quarter past nine	*It's quarter past nine.*
half past twelve	*It's half past twelve.*
twenty to six	*It's twenty to six.*

▶▶| **7** **Say the times in a different way. Listen to the example.**

It's nine thirty.
It's half past nine.

It's two fifteen.
It's quarter past two.

It's eight forty.
It's twenty to nine.

It's seven twenty.
It's twenty past seven.

It's twelve at night.
It's midnight.

It's twelve noon.
It's midday.

▶▶| **8** **Listen to the conversation.**

A Could I have two coffees, please?
B Yes. Anything else?
A Yes, could I have two hotdogs, please?
B Twelve euros sixty, please.

Listen again and repeat.

Unit 3

▶▶ 9 Listen to the conversation.

A What do you do?
B *I'm an engineer.*
A What company do you work for?
B *I work for ZY Systems.*
A OK, and where do you work?
B *I work in Washington.*
A Do you live there?
B *Yes, I live in Washington.*

Listen again and reply for you.

▶▶ 10 Say what you do and where you work. Listen to the example.

accountant / office
I'm an accountant. I work in an office.
engineer / factory
I'm an engineer. I work in a factory.
manager / warehouse
I'm a manager. I work in a warehouse.
receptionist / hotel
I'm a receptionist. I work in a hotel.
sales assistant / shop
I'm a sales assistant. I work in a shop.
technician / lab
I'm a technician. I work in a lab.

▶▶ 11 Listen to the conversation.

A What does your company do?
B *It makes products for the home.*
A Does it have suppliers in the UK?
B *No, it buys from suppliers in Sweden.*
A Does it have factories in the UK?
B *No, it has factories in Germany.*

Listen again and reply for you.

▶▶ 12 Listen to the conversation.

A What time do you get up in the morning?
B *I get up at quarter to six.*
A What do you have for breakfast?
B *I just have a coffee.*
A What time do you start work?
B *I start work at half past six.*
A When do you have lunch?
B *I have lunch at one o'clock.*
A When do you finish work?
B *I finish work at six.*

Listen again and reply for you.

Unit 4

►► 13 Listen and repeat.

What does B2B stand for?

What does 'Business to Business' mean?

How do you spell 'information'?

Do you understand English?

►► 14 Listen to the telephone conversation.

A Good morning. CCC, Christine speaking.

B *Could I speak to Sally Banks, please?*

A Yes, certainly. Who's calling, please?

B *Fergal Madden.*

A Could you say that again, please?

B *Fergal Madden.*

A Could you spell that, please?

B *Madden. M-A-D-D-E-N.*

A Thanks.

Listen again and reply. Ask to speak to Sally Banks.

►► 15 Ask questions. Listen to the example.

Tom's phone number

What's Tom's phone number?

Anne's extension number

What's Anne's extension number?

Mark's email address

What's Mark's email address?

The number of the London office

What's the number of the London office?

Mandy's mobile number

What's Mandy's mobile number?

The fax number of ZY Holdings

What's the fax number of ZY Holdings?

►► 16 Make sentences. Listen to the example.

work here / office

I	*I work here. This is my office.*
You	*You work here. This is your office.*
He	*He works here. This is his office.*
She	*She works here. This is her office.*
We	*We work here. This is our office.*
They	*They work here. This is their office.*

►► 17 Listen and repeat.

You can download the file.

You can buy tickets on the Internet.

You can call France from this phone.

I can't print the file.

We can't open the document.

He can't make a photocopy.

Transcripts

Unit 5

►►| 18 Ask questions. Listen to the example.

printer
Is there a printer?
photocopier
Is there a photocopier?
power sockets
Are there power sockets?
phone sockets
Are there phone sockets?
laptop
Is there a laptop?
drinks machine
Is there a drinks machine?

Listen and answer the questions about your office.

►►| 19 Say what you need to do. Listen to the example.

photocopy this document
I need to photocopy this document.
send an email
I need to send an email.
phone my office
I need to phone my office.
fax this
I need to fax this.
download this file
I need to download this file.
print this document
I need to print this document.

►►| 20 Make requests. Listen to the example.

could I use / fax machine
Could I use the fax machine?
computer
Could I use the computer?
photocopier
Could I use the photocopier?
printer
Could I use the printer?
phone

Could I use the phone?
your mobile
Could I use your mobile?

►►| 21 Ask for directions. Listen to the example.

excuse me / toilets
Excuse me, where are the toilets?
lift
Excuse me, where's the lift?
stairs
Excuse me, where are the stairs?
drinks machine
Excuse me, where's the drinks machine?
photocopier
Excuse me, where's the photocopier?

►►| 22 Listen to the conversation.

A Do you live in the town centre?
B *No, my apartment's about five kilometres from here.*
A Right. Do you live in a house or an apartment?
B *An apartment. It's quite small, just one bedroom.*
A Do you have a garden?
B *No, but the view is beautiful.*

Listen again and reply for you.

►►| 23 Make sentences. Listen to the example.

live
My house is quite old.
I live in quite an old house.
My apartment's very modern.
I live in a very modern apartment.
My apartment's quite small.
I live in quite a small apartment.
My house is very expensive.
I live in a very expensive house.
My house is quite big.
I live in quite a big house.

Unit 6

▶▶ 24 Listen and repeat.

She has a lot of meetings.
I don't often go abroad on business.
He always goes to the company
conference.
She doesn't make a lot of phone calls.
They never go to trade fairs.
We give a lot of presentations.

▶▶ 25 Listen to the questions and answers.

Do you often go on business trips?
I sometimes go on business trips, but not very often.
Do you often give presentations?
No, I never give presentations.
Do you often travel abroad?
No, I don't often travel abroad.
Do you usually finish work late?
Yes, I always finish late!
Do you usually have a lot of meetings?
Yes, I usually have a meeting every day.

Listen again and reply for you.

▶▶ 26 Make questions in the present continuous. Listen to the example.

What do you do?
What are you doing now?
What does he do?
What's he doing now?
Do you work in London?
Are you working in London now?
Does she work in London?
Is she working in London now?
Do you phone abroad?
Are you phoning abroad now?
Do they phone abroad?
Are they phoning abroad now?

Do you have lunch in a café?
Are you having lunch in a café now?
Does he have lunch in a café?
Is he having lunch in a café now?

▶▶ 27 Make sentences with *go*, *play*, or *do*. Listen to the example.

cycling	*I go cycling.*
swimming	*I go swimming.*
aerobics	*I do aerobics.*
chess	*I play chess.*
walking	*I go walking.*
football	*I play football.*
fishing	*I go fishing.*
weight training	*I do weight training.*
the guitar	*I play the guitar.*
skiing	*I go skiing.*

Transcripts

Unit 7

▶▶| 28 **Ask questions. Listen to the example.**

are you free / January
Are you free in January?
Friday
Are you free on Friday?
the fifteenth
Are you free on the fifteenth?
middle of May
Are you free in the middle of May?
the beginning of March
Are you free at the beginning of April?
the afternoon
Are you free in the afternoon?
four o'clock
Are you free at four o'clock?
July
Are you free in July?
the end of June
Are you free at the end of June?

▶▶| 29 **Listen to the conversation.**

A When are you going on your next business trip?
B *Next week. I'm leaving on Tuesday.*
A Where are you going?
B *To London. To visit a new customer.*
A Who are you meeting?
B *I'm seeing the sales manager of FB Products.*
A How are you travelling?
B *I'm taking the train.*
A Oh, right.

Listen again and reply for you.

▶▶| 30 **Ask questions about plans. Listen to the example.**

when / leave	*When are you leaving?*
who / meet	*Who are you meeting?*
how / travel	*How are you travelling?*
where / stay	*Where are you staying?*
why / go	*Why are you going?*

▶▶| 31 **Listen to the conversation.**

A Hello. Can I help you?
B *Yes. I'd like to book two tickets to Manchester, please.*
A When are you travelling?
B *Tomorrow.*
A What time?
B *At six o'clock in the evening.*
A Would you like to travel first class or standard class?
B *First class, please.*
A And would you like a single or a return?
B *A single, please.*
A Right. That's sixty five pounds forty, please.

Listen again and reply for you. Book two tickets to Manchester.

Unit 8

▶▶ 32 Make sentences. Listen to the example.

rade fair last week

    I was at a trade fair last week.

e   *He was at a trade fair last week.*

he   *She was at a trade fair last week.*

ve   *We were at a trade fair last week.*

hey   *They were at a trade fair last week.*

▶▶ 33 Make sentences. Listen to the example.

onference last year

    wasn't at the conference last year.

e

e wasn't at the conference last year.

he

he wasn't at the conference last year.

e

e weren't at the conference last year.

ney

ey weren't at the conference last year.

▶▶ 34 Ask questions. Listen to the example.

am meeting yesterday

ou

ere you at the team meeting yesterday?

e

as he at the team meeting yesterday?

he

as she at the team meeting yesterday?

ney

ere they at the team meeting yesterday?

▶▶ 35 Make sentences in the ast simple. Listen to the example.

ork on Wednesday

    I worked on Wednesday.

e   *He worked on Wednesday.*

e   *We worked on Wednesday.*

ey   *They worked on Wednesday.*

stay in a hotel

I   *I stayed in a hotel.*

he   *He stayed in a hotel.*

we   *We stayed in a hotel.*

they   *They stayed in a hotel.*

present the project

I   *I presented the project.*

He   *He presented the project.*

We   *We presented the project.*

They   *They presented the project.*

▶▶ 36 Make negative sentences. Listen to the example.

I presented the project.
I didn't present the project.

She talked about the prices.
She didn't talk about the prices.

We discussed the suppliers.
We didn't discuss the suppliers.

They visited the factory.
They didn't visit the factory.

He looked at the new production line.
He didn't look at the new production line.

I received the email yesterday.
I didn't receive the email yesterday.

▶▶ 37 Listen to the conversation.

A Hi. Where did go on holiday?

B *Paris.*

A Did you fly?

B *No, I took the train.*

A How long did you go for?

B *For a week.*

A What did you do?

B *We went sightseeing. And in the evenings we went to restaurants.*

A Did you have a good time?

B *Yeah, it was great.*

A Good.

Listen again and reply for you.

Unit 9

►►| 38 Listen and repeat the telephone expressions.

Hello. Could I speak to Lisa, please?
Hello. Is that Tony?
I'll call back later.
Could you ask her to call me back?

►►| 39 Answer questions about the weather. Listen to the example.

What's the weather like today?
rain
It's raining.
snow
It's snowing.
cold
It's cold.
sunny
It's sunny.

What's the weather usually like in November?
rain
It usually rains.
snow
It usually snows.
windy
It's usually windy.
foggy
It's usually foggy.

What was the weather like yesterday?
rain
It rained.
snow
It snowed.
cloudy
It was cloudy.
thunderstorm
There was a thunderstorm.

Unit 10

▶ 40 Say the comparatives.

pensive	more expensive
eap	cheaper
gh	higher
w	lower
onomical	more economical
od	better
d	worse
ort	shorter
ngerous	more dangerous
fe	safer
g	bigger
all	smaller
	further
sy	easier
ficult	more difficult

▶ 41 Say the comparatives and perlatives.

od	better	the best
eap	cheaper	the cheapest
nvenient	more convenient	the most convenient
pensive	more expensive	the most expensive
g	bigger	the biggest
sy	easier	the easiest
d	worse	the worst
st	faster	the fastest

▶▶ 42 Listen to the conversation at an airport.

A Hello. Can I have your ticket, please?
B *Yes, here you are.*
A Thank you. Do you have any identification?
B *Yes. My passport.*
A Thanks. An aisle or a window seat?
B *A window seat, please.*
A OK. Do you have any luggage?
B *I have one suitcase.*
A Any hand luggage?
B *Just a briefcase.*
A OK, fine. Here's your boarding pass. Boarding is in forty minutes. Gate ten C.
B *Thank you.*

Listen again and reply for you.

Unit 11

▶▶ 43 Make suggestions. Listen to the example.

Shall we plan the meeting?
Let's plan the meeting.
Shall we meet in Paris?
Let's meet in Paris.
Shall we talk again?
Let's talk again.
Shall we do that?
Let's do that.
Shall we go now?
Let's go now.

▶▶ 44 Ask questions about plans. Listen to the example.

next week
What are you doing next week?
tomorrow
What are you doing tomorrow?
this afternoon
What are you doing this afternoon?
on Wednesday
What are you doing on Wednesday?
next month
What are you doing next month?
tonight
What are you doing tonight?

▶▶ 45 Make sentences with *have got*. Listen to the example.

I have a reservation.
I've got a reservation.
Do you have your key?
Have you got your key?
I don't have the number.
I haven't got the number.
He has a minibar in his room.
He's got a minibar in his room.
She has a message from the office.
She's got a message from the office.

Unit 12

▶▶ 46 Make opposite sentences. Listen to the example.

The company's doing quite badly. / well
The company's doing quite well.
The market's growing fast. / slowly
The market's growing slowly.
We made a lot of money. / lost
We lost a lot of money.
We're making a profit. / loss
We're making a loss.
Sales increased by ten percent. / decreased
Sales decreased by ten percent.

▶▶ 47 Ask questions. Listen to the example.

How many / competitors
How many competitors are there?
stores
How many stores are there?
products
How many products are there?
How much competition
How much competition is there?
demand
How much demand is there?
interest
How much interest is there?

▶▶ 48 Listen and repeat.

Where's the changing room?
Can I try this on?
Are these shoes in the sale?
How much does this cost?
How much is this T-shirt?
Can I pay by credit card?

Answer key

Unit 1

1 1 c 2 a 3 d 4 b

2 1 We're 2 He's 3 They're
4 I'm 5 is, She's

3 1 Where's Bill from? He's from
London in the UK.
2 Where's Anna from? She's from
Hong Kong in China.
3 Where are Max and Anton from?
They're from Berlin in Germany.
4 Where's Sophie from? She's from
Paris in France.

4 *(any order)*
1 Are you from Paris?
2 Where are you from?
3 Would you like a coffee?
4 I'd like a mineral water.

5 a 1 Barcelona 2 Faro
3 Santander 4 Malaga
5 Toulon 6 Madrid

b 1 in the west of France
2 in the north-west of Portugal
3 in the north-east of France
4 in the north-west of France
5 in the south-east of France
6 in the west of Portugal

6 1 coffee 2 milk 3 orange juice
4 apple juice 5 mineral water
6 iced tea

7 1 sugar 2 no 3 please 4 this
5 country 6 mineral 7 welcome
8 an 9 sure 10 yes 11 right
12 thanks

8 1 Where are you from?
2 Where's that/Evry?
3 Where's Chuck from?
4 Are you from ZY Holdings?

5 Would you like a drink?
6 (Would you like) milk and suga

Unit 2

1

0 zero 1 one 2 two 3 three
4 four 5 five 6 six 7 seven
8 eight 9 nine 10 ten

2 1 nine nine nine 2 double oh
seven 3 ten 4 one 5 five

3 1 e 2 d 3 f 4 c 5 a 6 b

4 1 What's your number?
2 My mobile?
3 No, your office number.
4 Oh three four seven nine eight.
5 Nine eight?
6 That's right.

5

6 1 h, i 2 g, d 3 f 4 b 5 c
6 g, e

54

7 **1** am **2** midnight **3** time
4 eleven **5** night **6** to
7 o'clock

8 **1** What's your telephone number?
2 What time is it?
3 It's half past ten.
4 A tuna sandwich, please.
5 Two cheese sandwiches and a hot dog.
6 When's the next train to London?

Unit 3

1 **workplaces:** shop, factory, warehouse, office, hotel
jobs: receptionist, accountant, technician, engineer, manager

2 *(any order)*
1 He works for HMS.
2 Where do you live?
3 Do you live in Rome?
4 We live in London.
5 What do you do?
6 The company has two factories.

3 **1** He's Bruno Evans. He's an engineer.
2 He's Ed Nelson. He's a sales manager.
3 She's Maria Nock. She's an accountant.
4 She's Anne Nott. She's a technician.

4 **1** Hello. I'm Simon Fisher.
2 Nice to meet you, Simon. I'm Jan Bending.
3 What do you do, Jan?
4 I work for SHS. I'm a sales assistant.
5 In their London shop?
6 Yes, and where do you work, Simon?
7 I'm the manager for TopSport in Stuttgart.

5 **1** One thousand, three hundred and ninety pounds
2 Forty-eight thousand, one hundred and ninety-five euros.
3 One hundred and eighty thousand, six hundred and two pounds
4 One million, five hundred and sixty-seven thousand euros

6 **1** is **2** owns **3** have **4** make
5 works **6** buy

7 *(example answers)*
Oliver
He gets up early.
He has breakfast at quarter past six (in the morning).
He starts work at half past seven (in the morning).
He has lunch at midday/noon.
He finishes work at half past five (in the afternoon).
He has dinner at seven o'clock (in the evening).

Rachel
She gets up late.
She starts work at nine o'clock (in the evening).
She has lunch at two o'clock (in the afternoon).
She finishes work at six o'clock (in the morning).
She has dinner at half past eight (in the evening).

8 **1** I get up at six o'clock.
2 He has breakfast in a café.
3 When do you start work?
4 Where does she have lunch?
5 What company do they work for?
6 We have dinner at eight o'clock.

Answer key

Unit 4

1
1 What 2 How 3 What
4 Could 5 Does

2
1 receive 2 know 3 mean
4 email 5 could 6 understand
7 file 8 copy 9 again
10 stand 11 write 12 slowly
13 think

3
1 What's his job? He's an engineer.
2 She works in France. Her office is in Paris.
3 I live in the town centre. My address is 4, Station Street.
4 They live in France on the coast. Their home is in Cannes.
5 Is this your phone number? No, it's Jack's.
6 Our company has five factories. We make products for the home.

4
1 To 2 From 3 Subject
4 Dear 5 Thank 6 Best
7 Email 8 Tel. 9 Extension

5
1 software 2 website 3 mail
4 send 5 book 6 download
7 credit card 8 copy
9 hard drive 10 print

6
1 How do you spell that?
2 Could you speak slowly, please?
3 What's Jan's number?
4 What's the number of the Paris office?
5 I can't open the file.
6 You can download music from the Internet.

Unit 5

1
1 table 2 fax machine
3 photocopier 4 flip chart
5 printer 6 chairs

2
1 There are 2 There isn't
3 There are 4 There aren't
5 There's / There is 6 There are
7 There isn't 8 There aren't

3
laptop

4
1 door 2 bathroom 3 window
4 swimming pool 5 studio
6 exit 7 entrance 8 view
9 property 10 basement

5
1 old 2 low 3 big/large
4 nice 5 hot 6 cheap

6
1 Is there a photocopier?
2 There aren't phone sockets in the room.
3 I need to phone my office.
4 The toilets are over there on the right.
5 The rooms are very big.
6 My office is on the sixth floor.

7
1 the meeting room 2 the toilet
3 the interview room 4 the lift
5 the mail room

Unit 6

1
1 foreign 2 country
3 team 4 business 5 travel
6 conference 7 abroad 8 project
9 communication 10 world
11 Internet 12 presentations
13 colleague

2
1 He never goes on business trips.
2 We often go to conferences.
3 I am always in the office in the afternoon.
4 She doesn't usually give presentations in English.
5 They sometimes have meetings in my office.

3
1 Two men are speaking on the phone at the moment.
2 One man is/'s eating a sandwich.
3 One man is/'s working at a computer.
4 One woman is/'s writing a report.
5 One man is/'s reading a newspaper.
6 One woman is/'s making a photocopy.
7 Two people are drinking coffee.
8 One woman is/'s sending a fax.

4
1 cycling 2 chess 3 skiing
4 fishing 5 running 6 weight
training 7 golf 8 swimming

5
1 He doesn't often go cycling.
2 She never plays chess.
3 They sometimes play the guitar.
4 I usually do aerobics after work.
5 We never do weight training.

6
1 's/is 2 lot 3 are 4 like
5 playing 6 at 7 at 8 this

Unit 7

1
1 September 2 October
3 January 4 August 5 March
6 November 7 February 8 June
9 July 10 December 11 May
12 April

2
1 Friday 2 Monday 3 Sunday
4 Tuesday 5 Thursday
6 Saturday 7 Wednesday

3
at: the end of January, the beginning of the week, night, the end of the month
on: the 6th, the 10th, Monday, the 21st August
in: the afternoon, April, July, the middle of the month

4
1 d 2 c 3 e 4 a 5 b

5
1 d When's he leaving?
2 e How's she travelling?
3 b Is she flying direct?
4 a When are you coming back?
5 f Are you taking the train?
6 h Where are they staying?
7 c Who are they meeting?
8 g Why is she going by train?

6
1 timetable 2 reservation
3 fare 4 seat 5 return
6 first 7 book 8 single

7
1 I'm free at the beginning of the month.
2 Are you busy on Monday?
3 What are you doing next week?
4 I'm taking the train to Paris next Monday.
5 I want to travel first class.
6 I'd like to book a seat.

Unit 8

1
1 a hundred years ago
2 ten years ago
3 last year
4 last month
5 a week ago
6 three days ago
7 yesterday
8 this morning
9 this afternoon
10 this evening
11 tomorrow

Answer key

2
1 He wasn't at the meeting.
2 They were in India.
3 She was at the trade fair.
4 Were you at the training course?
5 They weren't in the office last week.
6 We were late this morning.
7 Was the meeting very big?

3
1 f How was the meeting?
2 d How many companies were at the trade fair?
3 a When was the conference?
4 c Who was at the training course?
5 e Where was the conference?
6 b Was the conference very big?

4
Hi Josh,
I'm back in the office again after my trip to Milan. The conference was fantastic. There were lots of very good talks and presentations. There was also a very good exhibition with lots of new books and new technology. It was a really big conference with over 3,000 visitors. Here is a copy of my report for your information.
Regards,
Tony

5 *(any order)*
1 His talk started at nine o'clock.
2 She travelled on business to China.
3 He worked all morning on the new project.
4 He stayed in a hotel near the airport.
5 Their presentation finished early.

6

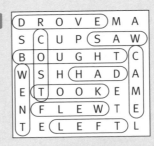

1 left 2 flew 3 bought
4 came 5 had 6 took 7 cost
8 drove 9 went 10 saw

7
1 holiday 2 apartment 3 beac
4 nightlife 5 coach 6 ferry
7 sightseeing 8 hotel

8
1 Did you rent a car?
2 When did you fly to Goa?
3 How did you travel?
4 How long did you stay in Paris?
5 Did he go to China last month?
6 Did they have a good holiday?

Unit 9

1 **Information**
in numbers: graph, bar chart, pie chart
in words: agenda, minutes, schedule
in numbers or words: table

2
1 Could you send me an email?
2 What time can I phone them?
3 I emailed Tom and sent him a copy of the report.
4 I called her at the office.
5 I need a copy of the minutes. Could you send one to me?
6 We need to discuss this with you. Could you call us?
7 Where are Sam and Tony? I need to speak to them.

3 1 hold 2 again 3 message
4 afraid 5 (across) back, (down)
busy 6 give 7 speak 8 calling
9 take/have 10 line

4 (any order)
1 I think taking a person's name
is quite easy. 2 I think taking
a message for a colleague is very
difficult. 3 Taking a person's
phone number is quite difficult.
4 Asking a person to call back
is very easy.

5 1 freezing 2 raining 3 foggy
4 sunny 5 snowing 6 windy

6 1 The weather was horrible last
night.
2 It rained all day yesterday.
3 It's snowing at the moment.
4 What's / What is the weather
like?
5 In April we often get a lot of
rain.
6 Last week it was windy and
cold.
7 In Moscow it's / it is freezing
today.
8 There was a thunderstorm in
Orlando last week.

Unit 10

1 1 modern 2 easy 3 expensive
4 short 5 good 6 fast 7 low
8 safe 9 large

M	S	H	O	R	T	V	E	M
A	D	D	O	O	F	I	L	O
N	E	E	S	E	A	S	Y	D
E	X	P	E	N	S	I	V	E
L	L	O	W	E	T	S	O	R
G	O	O	D	E	R	A	K	N
O	N	E	E	L	A	F	I	N
M	P	L	A	R	G	E	S	G

2 1 A train is longer than a bus.
2 A Ford is cheaper than a
Rolls Royce.
3 This old fax machine is worse
than that new one.
4 Economy class is less expensive
than business class.
5 A sports car can go faster than a
bus.
6 This modern laptop is smaller
than that computer.
7 This is the most difficult
question in the book!
8 You always have the best ideas.

3 1 agree 2 think 3 sure
4 right 5 true

4 1 Twenty years ago planes were the
most expensive way to travel.
2 Today the fastest way to travel
from London to Paris is by train.
3 The TGV is the quickest way to
travel between cities in France.
4 The most convenient way to
travel is by car.
5 The least comfortable way to
travel for long distances is by
bus.

5 1 N 2 N 3 N 4 S 5 N 6 S
1 The flight to Berlin is now
boarding. The flight is on time. /
The flight to Berlin isn't
boarding. The flight is delayed.
2 The flight to London is cancelled.
The check-in is closed. / The
flight to London isn't cancelled.
The check-in is now open.
3 The Paris flight is delayed. It's
thirty minutes late. / The Paris
flight is on time. It isn't late.
5 There's no flight to Bangkok.
Passengers aren't getting onto
the plane. / There's a flight to
Bangkok. Passengers are getting
onto the plane.

Answer key

6 1 any 2 any, some 3 any, no
4 any, some 5 any, no

7 1 to 2 more 3 The 4 on
5 than 6 not

Unit 11

1 1 First 2 After 3 Then
4 Finally 5 next

2 *(any order)*
1 Let's talk about the date of the next meeting.
2 Shall we work on the brochure or discuss the prices?
3 Where shall we have our next meeting?
4 Shall I call you this afternoon?
5 When shall we have dinner?

3 1 photos 2 website 3 product
4 next 5 date 6 urgent
7 important 8 after

4 1 They're going to look at the brochure next/this week.
2 Are you going to make changes to the website?
3 He's going to discuss the new project tomorrow.
4 They're going to call the office later.
5 We're not going to have the design ready for the meeting.

5 1 I've got a reservation for a double room.
2 Could you fill in this form, please?
3 Can you put your signature here, please?
4 This card is the key for your room.
5 Would you like a wake-up call?
6 Could I check out, please?
7 My company's paying the bill.

6 1 Hello. We've got a reservation for two single rooms.
2 Could you tell me your names, please?
3 Sure. Briggs and Wood.
4 For two nights?
5 Yes, that's right.
6 Could you fill in this form, please?
7 Of course.
8 OK. Rooms 203 and 204 on the second floor. Here are your key:
9 Thanks.

7 1 've/have 2 Have 3 haven't
4 's/has/hasn't 5 've/have

8 1 d check out 2 f bill
3 a minibar 4 e credit card
5 c extras 6 g room service
7 b receptionist

Unit 12

1 1 increased 2 quarter 3 profit
margin 4 decreased 5 sales
6 loss 7 costs 8 improve

2 1 many 2 many 3 much
4 much 5 much 6 many

3 1 At the moment our company is doing quite badly.
2 My colleagues work very hard. My colleague works very hard.
3 Business improved quickly last year.
4 It's not good for businesses to grow fast/quickly.
5 Our sales are increasing slowly

4 1 compete 2 demand
3 competitors 4 supermarket
5 competition 6 competitive
7 profit 8 off 9 earn
10 discount 11 order 12 goo

5 1 those 2 this 3 these 4 that

6 1 sale 2 off 3 try, changing
4 size 5 cash 6 receipt
7 pin number 8 Medium

7 1 Do you need any help?

2 Yes, please. How much do these shoes cost? I can't find the price.

3 They're £50 now. They were £90.

4 Can I try them on?

5 Yes, of course. What's your size?

6 I'm a size 43. That's size 10 in the UK, I think.

7 Yes. That's right. Here you are. ... Are they OK?

8 Yes, fine. I'll take them. Can I pay by credit card?

9 Yes, no problem.

IRREGULAR VERBS

Infinitive	Past simple	Infinitive	Past simple
be	was/were	learn	learned/learnt
become	became	leave	left
begin	began	lose	lost
break	broke	make	made
bring	brought	meet	met
build	built	pay	paid
buy	bought	put	put
catch	caught	read	read /red/
choose	chose	ring	rang
come	came	run	ran
cost	cost	say	said
cut	cut	see	saw
do	did	sell	sold
draw	drew	send	sent
drink	drank	sing	sang
drive	drove	sleep	slept
eat	ate	speak	spoke
fall	fell	spend	spent
feel	felt	stand	stood
find	found	swim	swam
fly	flew	take	took
forget	forgot	teach	taught
get	got	tell	told
give	gave	think	thought
go	went	throw	threw
have	had	understand	understood
hear	heard /hɜːd/	wake	woke
keep	kept	wear	wore
know	knew	win	won
		write	wrote

cknowledgements

e **authors** would like to
:nowledge above all the significant
ntribution to the course made by
:halie and Aimy Ibbotson, and
;enia Miassoedova. They were a
nstant source of support and ideas
all stages of the project and
played remarkable patience!

anks also to: Will Capel for
ieving in the project and for his
/ice and expertise during the
ical early stages of development,
ly Searby for her encouragement
1 commitment to getting the best
: of the course, Clare Abbott for
excellent editorial input –
ecially in guiding the material
ough key improvements to the
cept and methodology, Elin Jones
her valuable editorial advice,
as and positive support – much
reciated during the intense phase
writing the first level, and Chris

Capper for his helpful input on the
early units. A big thanks to our editor
Nick Robinson, whose positive
energy, ideas and feel for the
material have been instrumental in
shaping the second level. And a
special thanks to our copy editor
Fran Banks, for giving *Business
Start-up* the benefit of her expertise,
eagle eyes and extremely hard work.

We would also like to thank the
many reviewers who have offered
valuable comments on the material
at various stages of development,
including Alex Case, Helen Forrest,
Radoslaw Lewandowski, Rosemary
Richey and Robert Szulc.

The publishers would like to thank
James Richardson and Studio AVP for
the audio production and Bee2 Ltd
for the CD-ROM development.

CD-ROM / Audio CD instructions

Audio CD instructions

Play the CD in a standard CD player. You can also play the CD on your computer:

1 Insert the disc into your CD-ROM drive.
2 The CD-ROM application will open automatically – if you do not want to run the application, close or minimise it.
3 Open your computer's CD player software (for example, Microsoft® Windows Media® Player).

CD-ROM instructions for PC

1 Insert the CD into your CD-ROM drive.
2 The program should start automatically.
3 If, after a few seconds, the program has not started, open 'My Computer', then browse to your CD-ROM drive and double-click on the 'START-UP' icon.

CD-ROM instructions for Mac OSX

1 Insert the CD into your CD-ROM drive.
2 Open the CD-ROM folder and double-click on the 'START-UP' icon.

System requirements

For PC

Recommended: Windows 2000 or XP, 400MHz processor or faster, with 128MB of RAM or more.

For Mac

Essential: Mac OSX, version 10.1 or higher.
Recommended: 400MHz G3 processor or better, with 128MB RAM or more.